# DILLON THE CHAMELEON
## Jurassic Survivor

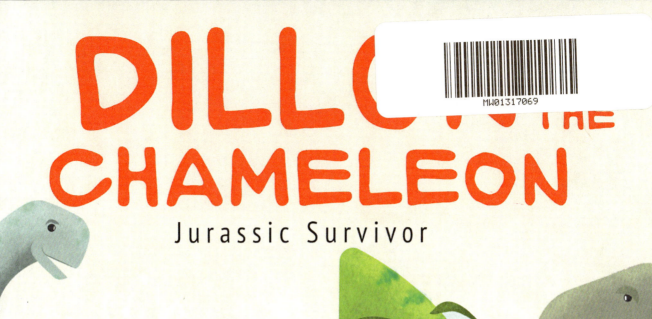

**ANDY PAVE**

*To my beloved wife:*
*your empathic support, trust and love*
*made this possible*

*- A.P.*

Copyright © 2020 by Andy Pave
All rights reserved.

This is a work of fiction. Names, characters, places, and incidents either are products of the author's imagination or are used
fictitiously. Any similarity to actual events or locales or persons, living or dead, is entirely coincidental.

No part of this publication may be reproduced, stored in or introduced into a retrieval system, or transmitted, in any form, or by any means (electronic, mechanical, photocopying, recording, or otherwise) without the prior written permission of the copyright owner.

# Dillon the Chameleon
## Jurassic Survivor

By Andy Pave

Original concept, text and storyboard by Andy Pave
Pictures by Joseba San Severino

Sixty five million years ago, a lizard called Dillon was happy with his own company.

All on his own, he happily snoozed on rocks.
I don't need friends, he thought.
I can take care of myself!

One day, Tim Pterodactyl flew over.
He shouted, "A huge snowfall is coming!"

The dinosaurs prepared for the storm.
They helped one another build shelters.

But Dillon had no friends to help him.

Coldness gripped the land.
Snow fell endlessly.

Now I wish I had friends to help me, Dillon thought. If I stay here, I will freeze.

He tried to push a rock to make a shelter, but it would not budge.

Lex T-Rex said, "You can't possibly carry that rock. Are you crazy?"

Lex's friends laughed. Dillon felt weak, angry, and helpless. He thought, I don't need them!

Ben Brontosaurus stood tall, watching the storm.

Dillon shouted, "Will you lift me up so I can see?" But Ben ignored him.

Tyler Triceratops had gathered coconuts for food.

Dillon said, "Can I spend the storm in your lair?"

Tyler exclaimed, "No! I could run out of coconuts! Why should I share with you?"

Dillon felt very afraid and lonely.
I don't need Tyler, he thought.

His short legs sank into the snow, and he felt so cold.

He muttered, "I'll go to the lake for a drink."

The lake was frozen.

Dillon stared at his reflection, feeling lost and small.

He shed a tear that froze and fell onto the ice. *Ping!*

Suddenly, eyes moved under the ice. An orange fish looked at Dillon.

It said, "To make your coldness disappear, get rid of the coldness in your heart."

With all his strength, Dillon tried to understand what this meant.

The fish said, "The magic question is: **What is it like to be in your skin?**"

Dillon repeated:
**"What is it like to be in your skin?"**

Suddenly Dillon's skin turned orange like the fish's.

He was amazed!

By listening with his whole body,
and asking the magic question,
he could understand what others were feeling.

His skin could change color
and show him the emotions
of other animals!

Dillon shouted, "Thank you, Fish!"
With a flap, the fish disappeared.

Icy wind howled. Dillon wondered if the dinosaurs had completed their shelters.

If I had understood them better, Dillon thought, and been nicer, we could have survived together.

Maybe it's not too late for me to change.

Dillon bravely climbed back through the mountains.

Tyler Triceratops popped up from out of the fog.

Dillon said, "Will you share your coconuts?"

Tyler again replied, "No!"

Dillon remembered the fish's message and instead of criticizing Tyler, he listened with empathy, and remembered the magic question:

**What is it like to be in your skin?**

Dillon's own skin turned gray. He understood that Tyler was feeling fear.

Dillon said, "Please keep calm. After the storm, the sun will shine. There are more palm trees beyond the mountains and together we could gather more coconuts."

Tyler felt calmer. He gave Dillon a coconut and a hug.

Dillon walked on with a full stomach.

Meeting Ben again, he asked, "How does the storm look from up there?" Again, Ben ignored him.

Dillon remembered the fish's message, so instead of criticizing Ben, he tried to understand him. Dillon asked himself the magic question:

**What is it like to be in your skin?**

Suddenly, Dillon's skin turned blue. He said, "I believe that you feel sadness."

Ben looked surprised and answered, "Yes! I have been sad for many years because I am too tall to enjoy the colorful flowers. No one has ever understood me before. Thank you!"

Ben extended a leg for Dillon to climb. He carried Dillon to the next hill.

Later, Dillon met Lex T-Rex and his gang. Dillon called, "Would you help me carry this rock?"

Lex said, "Why would I help you, midget?"

Dillon was hurt.

It was hard not to criticize Lex, but he remembered the fish's message and did his best to ask himself the magic question:

**What is it like to be in your skin?**

Suddenly, Dillon's skin turned red.

He asked, "Are you angry?" Lex looked surprised, and replied, "Yes! Because the other tyrannosaurs tease me. They say I'm not strong enough. You showed me that anger has taken hold of me. Thank you."

Then Lex smiled and said, "Of course I'll carry that stone. Tell me where to put it." Lex pushed the rock onto a ledge.

Finally, I have a shelter, Dillon thought.

Suddenly the ledge cracked and the stone rolled into the valley.

Dillon moaned. That was my last hope of surviving, he thought. Now there's no hope and I will freeze.

Snow piled on him as he began to shiver.

Tania the Turtle peeked through the falling snow.

Dillon asked, "Why are you smiling when we're going to freeze?"

Tania answered, "My shell has grown larger. We can both fit in it until the cold passes."

Dillon was surprised. He didn't understand much about Tania, but he remembered the fish's message.

**What is it like to be in your skin?**

Dillon's skin turned golden!

He asked, "Tania, do you feel happy?"
She answered, "Yes, I am joyful when I can share. Now that I have this extra space, I want to share it with you."

Hiding inside, he understood he had a new superpower:

he could feel what others feel.

If he could feel their emotions, he could understand them better.

If he understood them, he could help them.

And if he helped them, his own life would get better and he'd have friends.

The storm was very powerful but finally it ended and wild flowers bloomed.

And this is how chameleons learned to change color. They practiced the magic question for millions of years and learned it very well. In fact, they still do it today!

If you pay attention, you might see one around asking another animal the magic question:

**What is it like to be in your skin?**

The End

# Let's keep learning with Dillon the Chameleon

Dear Parent / Teacher:
Here are some suggested questions that can be addressed in conversation with your young reader. This, in addition to providing a pleasant time between the two of you, can serve as a starting point for implementing the lessons and making positive changes in your children's lives.

## Questions for children:

1. What character names do you remember from this story?

2. Did you like any character more? Why?

3. What was the Magic Question that the fish gave Dillon?

4. What colors does Dillon's skin turn when the Magic Question is asked in front of each of the characters?

## Questions to be asked or rephrased by the parent to their child:

5. What does Dillon change in his dealings with the other characters after meeting the fish?

6. When Dillon took shelter in Tania the Turtle's house, what did he learn?

7. How was Tania with Dillon?

8. Would you like to be like Tania with your family and friends? If so, describe what you would be like.

9. When could you use the Magic Question at home or at your school?

10. Would you invent a new color or combination of colors to an emotion or feeling that you also have? If so, we would love to know!

Post your own drawing on social media using the hashtags #DillonTheChameleon and @andypavebooks.

You can also send us your drawing to andypavebooks@gmail.com with the title "My friend Dillon and me". We would love to receive it!

## QUESTIONS TO EXPLORE EMOTIONS, GUIDED BY PARENTS OR TEACHERS:

11. What person do you know who is like Lex T-Rex, Ben Brontosaur or Tyler Triceratops?
11.1 Now ask yourself the Magic Question with that person.
11.2 Take note of what you think that person feels.
11.3 How can you treat that person differently from your own answer?

12. What can you do when you feel like Lex T-Rex so as not to hurt the people you love?

13. What could you say to yourself when you feel like Ben Brontosaur to make yourself feel better?

14. Open a newspaper or magazine, choose a story from someone you don't know and ask yourself the Magic Question.

After you have answered, imagine that you have that person in front of you ... Quickly think of 3 ideas that could help to improve that person's life and write them down!

1._____

2._____

3._____

**Thank you for reading
Dillon the Chameleon
Jurassic Survivor!**

If you enjoyed this book,
I'd be **very grateful** if you'd post a short
review on Amazon.

Your support *really* does
make a difference.
I read all the reviews personally so I can
make future books for you even better.

**Thank you!**

Copyright © 2020 by Andy Pave
All rights reserved.

Made in United States
North Haven, CT
12 April 2022

18142508R00024